The Zodiac

The Vocabulary of Human Qualities and Characteristics

Mary Riddle Moore

PRO LINGUA ASSOCIATES

Pro Lingua Associates, Publishers
74 Cotton Mill Hill, Suite A315
Brattleboro, Vermont 05302 USA
Office: 802-257-7779
Orders: 800-366- 4775
Email: info@ProLinguaAssociates.com
WebStore www.ProLinguaAssociates.com
SAN: 216-0579

At Pro Lingua
our objective is to foster an approach
to learning and teaching that we call
***interplay**, the **inter**action of language*
learners and teachers with their materials,
with the language and culture,
and with each other in active, creative,
*and productive **play**.*

Text ISBN 978-0-86647-477-1
Audio CD ISBN 978-0-86647-478-8
Text/CD set ISBN 978-0-86647-479-5
Digital Edition ISBN 978-0-86647-480-1

The Zodiac was designed and set in Adobe Times New Roman by Arthur A. Burrows. This is a digital font based on an early twentieth-century old-fashioned serif type called Times New Roman, commissioned by the British newspaper *The Times* in 1931 and designed by Victor Lardent for the Monotype company. Digitized and distributed with Microsoft products, it has become one of the most widely used typefaces in history. It is easy to read, with strong contrasting bold and italic faces.

The front cover illustration is © by Caloncici; the dark sky © by Sergii Kateryniuck, both from Dreamstime.com. The illustrations on pages iii, ix, x, and 54 are by Robert MacLean, who illustrated the original edition. The other illustrations used throughout the book are from the Dreamstime.com Agency. The illustration on the title page is © by Pretendiendomucho, as are the small symbols used on the contents pages and the first page of each unit. Most of the illustrations in this edition are © by Kseniya Polishchuk, specifically those on pages xii, 3, 7, 11, 15, 19, 23, 27, 31, 32, 35, 39, 43, 45, 47, 48, 53, and 58. Work by other illustrators is on these pages: v © Pe3ak; 4, 12, 16, 46, 59 © Christos Georghiou; 8, 36 © Littlepaw; 20, 44 © Tatianakost; 24 © Minerias6; 28 © Dmitri Elmor; 40 © Patrick; 49 © Alenalazareva; the sea goat on the back cover and on 52 © Elena Shah.

The book was printed and bound by Royal Palm Press in Punta Gorda, Florida.

Printed in the United States of America
First printing, third edition 2018.

Foreword

Pro Lingua is pleased to bring back into print this vocabulary builder we first published in 1985. The author, known to us as "Franki," was an ESL teacher for the School for International Training at the Jacksonville and Brattleboro campuses. Unfortunately Franki passed away too soon Her book had been in print for over 25 years when other pressures caused us to let it go out of print temporarily. Finally we are pleased to bring it back to be enjoyed by today's teachers and students.

Dedication

To my mother, Elaine Riddle

Acknowledgements

My special thanks go to Candy Ball for her patience in typing the original draft. I would also like to express my appreciation to Ray Clark for his sound advice and support in the preparation of this book.

MRM, 1984

Pro Lingua would like to express our appreciation to Janie Duncan for the preparation of this second edition and to James Sweet, Franki's stepson, for his permission to revise and publish it.

Contents

Contents: Zodiac Lessons with Vocabulary

dignified	egotistical	materialistic
proud	domineering	cautious
vain	honest	bossy
overpowering		

perfect	thrifty	dependable
anxious	meticulous	gentle
inefficient	nervous	compassionate

calm	fair	sensible
gracious	indecisive	intelligent
harmonious	logical	extravagant
nasty	cranky	

brutal	intense	smart
courageous	emotional	talented
confident	secretive	jealous

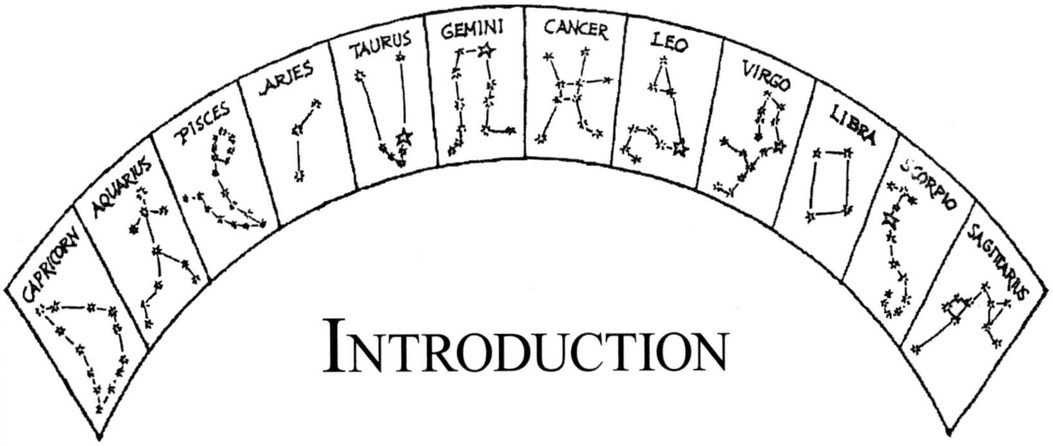

Introduction

The purpose of this book is to help learners of English develop their vocabulary in an efficient and enjoyable way. It is the first in a series of vocabulary texts published by Pro Lingua since 1984.*

As is obvious, the key words all relate to a lexical field: words, especially adjectives, that describe the qualities and characteristics of human beings. This grouping of words allows the learner to focus on words that, in one way or another, connect with each other. This interconnectedness allows the learner to develop their vocabulary systematically rather than randomly.

But why "The Zodiac"? Please understand that we are not publishing this book to endorse the field of astrology, but rather to use this ancient view of understanding human nature as a convenient, enjoyable way to learn words. And who hasn't taken a look at their horoscope to see what is in store for the day, believer or not?

* See the list of books on the last page of this book.

User's Guide

This book is a vocabulary development text that focuses on words which are descriptive of human qualities and characteristics. Most of these key words are first used as adjectives, but noun and verb forms of the words are also explored in the practice activities that follow the reading.

The recommended proficiency level is low intermediate with a vocabulary of about 600 words. Age level: middle school and up.

This second edition of *Zodiac* is a photocopyable teacher's resource. As such, it can be used in a number of ways, adapted as necessary to fit your teaching situation and your students. It can, of course, be used as a student text, with each student having a copy of the book. If it is used as a teacher resource, the basic procedure would be to use selected units on an occasional basis, once or twice a week with ongoing follow-up reviews.

Additional follow-up work focused on conversation is available and explained in the Appendices.

A basic procedure:

1. **Introduce the book**. Select one of the units (The zodiac begins with Aries, on the first day of spring.) and tell the learners the purpose of the unit. You can use the **Learner's Guide** following this introduction.

2. **List the key words** on the board or as a separate handout. See the table of contents for the words that will be the focus of the lesson.

3. **Explore the meanings** of the key words. Have the learners work in small groups to see if they know the meanings of the words.
   - Give them five minutes to work together.
   - Have each group report on what they know and do not know.
   - Focus on the "Don't Know" words and tell them to look for them in the reading.

4. For the very first unit, you **read the passage aloud**. This keeps everyone "on the same page." You can stop as you encounter each key word, but it is usually more effective to read the entire passage through without stopping; then go back to look at and discuss the form and meaning of each key word.

5. Have the learners **look at the famous people** and see who in the class might also be born under the sign.

6. Have the learners **do the exercises** in class or assign them as homework. If you do the exercises in class, as learners finish, pair them to compare each other's answers.

7. Hand out and go over the answers.

8. As you proceed through the book, recycle the fourth exercise (D) from previously done units.

Gemini Twins

LEARNER'S GUIDE

This book is a vocabulary development text that focuses on words about human qualities and characteristics. There are over 100 words. Most of these key words are first used as adjectives. But noun and verb forms of the words are also explored in the practice activities that follow the reading.

This special vocabulary is presented in twelve readings about the kinds of people who are born under the signs of the zodiac. You are not expected to believe the truthfulness of the descriptions. The use of the this book is simply to help make the learning of vocabulary more interesting and fun.

The passages are written in a way that will help you learn the meaning of each key word through the context – the thoughts that precede and follow the word. Although you may have to use a dictionary from time to time, you should first try to understand the words by studying the context. By doing this, you will also develop your reading skills.

The units are organized according to the following plan:

Reading: Each reading is a description of a typical person born under one of the signs of the zodiac. The key vocabulary is in **bold type**. Just for fun, at the end of the reading is a short list of famous people who were born under this sign.

Exercises: There are four exercises after each reading, so you can practice using each word and its forms (noun, verb, adjective).

March 21

Aries

April 19

The symbol of Aries is the ram. Like the ram, Arians are **aggressive**. They will attack a person they disagree with or an idea they dislike. They are extremely **decisive** and always know exactly what they want to do. Arians are so **energetic** that they rarely feel tired. They are very **ambitious**, wanting to succeed in life. Arians are **enthusiastic** about all their projects. They take great interest in them and will work on them day and night.

Arians are so decisive and honest that they seem **brash** at times. They will tell the truth even if it is painful to another person. However, Arians can also be **sympathetic** to people. They will try to understand and help others with their problems, but they are sometimes **impatient** with people who work or think slowly. They do not like to wait for anyone. Arians are **optimistic** about life. They believe that the future will always be better.

CAREER: Arians will enjoy professions that are exciting and that do not involve taking too many orders. They would be good explorers, research scientists, fire fighters or professional soldiers. They would probably like sports such as car racing, boxing, and tennis.

LOVE: Virgo, a **well-organized** person who gets things done, would be a good choice for a mate. Libra would also be a good match, as this sign is both sympathetic and intelligent. Arians should avoid other Arians, as their similar qualities will cause them to be **combative**. They will have many arguments and fights. Arians will be loyal partners unless they lose interest.

Famous Arians

Maya Angelou
Leonardo da Vinci
Elton John
Thomas Jefferson
Lady Gaga
Vincent van Gogh

A. Match the phrase in column A with a phrase in Column B.

A	B
1. A **combative** person _____	A) usually knows where everything is.
2. An **optimistic** person _____	B) would start an argument.
3. A **sympathetic** person _____	C) can hurt your feelings.
4. A **well-organized** person _____	D) will make up their mind quickly.
5. A **brash** person _____	E) does not like to wait.
6. An **enthusiastic** person _____	F) is usually a hard worker
7. An **aggressive** person _____	G) is a person who likes to fight.
8. An **ambitious** person _____	H) is understanding.
9. An **energetic** person _____	I) believes in the future.
10. A **decisive** person _____	J) is rarely tired.
11. An **impatient** person _____	K) is eager to do things.

B. Complete the sentences with one of the words below.

aggressive	enthusiastic	impatient	decisive
brash	optimistic	energetic	
combative	ambitious	sympathetic	

1. Ray thinks about a problem for a short time and then decides what to do. He is a _____________ person.
2. Stefan never gets tired. He's so _____________!
3. Marissa works hard and wants to make lots of money. She's an _____________ person.
4. Ricardo feels sorry for all the poor people in the world. He is a _____________ person.
5. Anita does not like to wait for anything or anyone. She is an _____________ person.
6. Juan always thinks tomorrow will be a better, happier day. He's an _____________ person.
7. Alex often starts arguments with his friends. He's a _____________ person.
8. Peter will talk to strangers or demand something if he wants it. He's an _____________ person.
9. Jerome likes to tell people exactly what he thinks about everything. Some people think he's a rude, _____________ person.
10. Mohamed is always very excited and happy about doing new things. He's an _____________ person.

C. Fill in the blank with the correct form of the key word.

1. Is Jose an energetic person? He's well known for his ____________y.
2. Is Pierre a sympathetic person? He's well known for his ____________y.
3. Is Takeshi an aggressive person? He's well known for his ____________ness.
4. Is Gustav a combative person? He's well known for enjoying ____________.
5. Is Ingrid an optimistic person? She's well known for her ____________ism.
6. Is Simone an impatient person? She's well known for her ____________ce.
7. Is Michelle a brash person? She's well known for her ____________ness.
8. Is Deniz an enthusiastic person? She's well known for her ____________sm.
9. Is Ayşe an ambitious person? She's well known for her ____________ion.
10. Is Sergio a decisive person? He's well known for his ____________ ness.

D. Match each word with its OPPOSITE meaning (antonym).

1. aggressive ______	A. not hopeful
2. decisive ______	B. messy
3. energetic ______	C. unfeeling
4. ambitious ______	D. peaceful
5. enthusiastic ______	E. tired
6. brash ______	F. willing to wait
7. well-organized ______	G. not eager
8. sympathetic ______	H. unable to decide
9. impatient ______	I. polite
10. combative ______	J. shy
11. optimistic ______	K. lazy

April 20

Taurus

May 20

The symbol for Taurus is the bull. Taureans are **strong** and **determined**. They have no respect for weakness of any kind. Although people admire their strength, they are sometimes angered by their determination. Nothing will stand between them and the goals they have set for themselves. Taureans can also be very **stubborn**, refusing to change their opinion or to do things that do not interest them. It does no good to argue with them. Once they have made up their mind, they will not change it. Taureans have many loyal friends. They are **generous** with both their time and money. In fact, they usually have a lot of cash and property, but they are not **stingy**. They love to buy expensive gifts for their family and friends. A Taurean will always help a friend. They will give money or take time to listen to another person's problems.

For Taureans, their home is their castle. They need a **serene** atmosphere. They hate loud noises and enjoy being surrounded by beautiful things. And they love to eat. As a result, average Taureans are not always **healthy,** because they can be **obese**. People born under the sign of Taurus must constantly watch their weight.

CAREER: Taureans are practical people who believe in solid foundations and security. They are often involved in fields such as banking, education, medicine, engineering, and food production.

LOVE: A Pisces is a good choice for a Taurean. This sign generally has a peaceful nature and also will appreciate a Taurean's strength. An Arian is too nervous and fast-moving for the **deliberate** Taurean. A Taurean always thinks things out slowly and carefully before making a decision.

Famous Taureans

George Clooney	Tina Fey	David Beckham
Adele	Dev Patel	William Shakespeare

A. Match the phrase in column A with a phrase in column B.

A	B
1. People who are **stubborn** _____	A) try hard to achieve their goals.
2. People who are **generous** _____	B) are selfish.
3. People who are **serene** _____	C) are not easily injured or defeated.
4. People who are **determined** _____	D) refuse to change their minds.
5. People who are **obese** _____	E) are peaceful.
6. People who are **stingy** _____	F) are not often sick.
7. People who are **deliberate** _____	G) are happy to share what they have.
8. People who are **strong** _____	H) are fat.
9. People who are **healthy** _____	I) make careful decisions.

B. Complete the sentence with one of the words below.

obese	strength	determined
stubbornness	deliberate	generosity
stingy	serenity	healthy

1. Although Harry knew he was wrong, his ___________ kept him from changing his mind.
2. Yusef works overtime every day in the office. He is _____________ to be the president of the company someday.
3. Maria gives a lot of money to help poor people. She's known for her _____________.
4. Poor Jeanne can never stay on a diet. She's very worried about being _____________.
5. Mr. Scrooge was a very selfish man. Everyone knew he was very _________________.
6. I like to walk on quiet, uncrowded beaches. I can find _____________ there.
7. Yoshi does not like weakness. He admires _____________.
8. Ray takes a long time to make important decisions. In fact, he is very _____________.
9. Pedro is never sick . He is very ______________.

C. Fill in each blank with the correct form of the word in bold type.

1. **Stingy** people are known for their ___________ .
2. **Obese** people suffer from ___________ .
3. **Deliberate** people are known for their ___________ .
4. **Serene** people enjoy ___________ .
5. **Generous** people are known for their ___________ .
6. **Stubborn** people are known for their ___________ .
7. **Determined** people are known for their ___________ .
8. **Strong** people have a lot of ___________ .
9. **Healthy** people have good ___________ .

D. Match the words in column A with an OPPOSITE meaning in column B.

A	B
1. stingy ______	a. changeable, flexible
2. obese ______	b. sick
3. deliberate ______	c. noisy
4. serene ______	d. weak
5. stubborn ______	e. thin
6. healthy ______	f. impulsive or careless
7. strong ______	g. generous

May 21 ← # Gemini → June 20

The symbol for Gemini is twins, two sisters or brothers born at the same time. The twins represent the two sides of Gemini's personality and also their **fickle** nature. Geminis often change their mind about things. Despite their fickleness, they are much loved by their friends because they are **charming**. Geminis always know the right thing to say and do. They are also **witty**, often making clever, funny comments.

Geminis are not **malicious**. They would never do anything to hurt someone. However, sometimes they do hurt people without meaning to do so because they are very **competitive**, always trying to be the best at everything they do. They work quickly and well; however, they hate **monotonous** work. Doing the same thing over and over is very boring to them. Constant change suits their **restless** nature. They are always looking for new and exciting things to do. However, they need to be careful, because the health of Geminis is often **delicate**, not very strong.

CAREER: The best professions for Geminis involve communication. They excel as journalists, lecturers, teachers, and authors. Their ability to communicate and entertain helps them greatly in these fields.

LOVE: Geminis are often accused of fickleness, because they are capable of loving many people at the same time. It is difficult for them to be loyal to only one partner. They should avoid a sign such as Taurus, whose love of home life would seem **mundane** and too ordinary for them. Being with another Gemini is best, since they will truly understand each other.

Famous Geminis

John F. Kennedy	Angelina Jolie	Rafael Nadal
Kanye West	Morgan Freeman	Donald Trump

A. Match the word in bold type with its definition.

1. A **restless** person _____	A) gets sick easily.
2. A **witty** person ____	B) is very ordinary.
3. A **delicate** person _____	C) is very changeable.
4. A **fickle** person _____	D) likes to move around.
5. A **monotonous** life _____	E) makes jokes.
6. A **malicious** person _____	F) likes to win.
7. A **mundane** life _____	G) is unkind to others.
8. A **competitive** person _____	H) is usually liked by others.
9. A **charming** person _____	I) is not very exciting.

B. Fill in the blank with the correct word.

1. Did John take Alice to the party last night? No, he took Jane. He's so _____________. He changes girlfriends every week.

2. Let's invite Hans to the party. The guests will enjoy him. He's so funny. Hans is a _____________ person.

3. Kim often says cruel things about her friends. I really don't like her. She's definitely a ____________ ious person.

4. Phil never changes his routine. He does the same thing every day. His life must certainly be ____________ ous.

5. Harlan never stays in one place for a long time. He loves to travel. He certainly is a _____________ person.

6. Abdullah has a bad cold. He catches cold easily. His health is very _____________.

7. Mary likes to cook and to clean her house. She isn't interested in travel or adventure. Some people think she has a _____________ life.

8. People love Paulo. He's so polite and understanding. What a _____________ man he is!

9. Annie is a great runner. She hates to lose. She is a very _____________ person.

C. Choose a key word that completes the sentence.

1. Is John a faithful boyfriend?

   Certainly not! He's well known for his ____________ ness.

2. Is television exciting?

   Certainly not! It's very ____________ ous.

3. Is Herbert a quiet child?

   Certainly not! He's well known for his ____________ ness.

4. Is Robert a kind man?

   Certainly not! He's well known for his ____________ ness.

5. Is Jay a boring person?

   Certainly not! He's very ____________ ing.

6. Is Gerry a strong person?

   Certainly not! He's well known for his ____________ ness.

7. Is Charlotte a dull person?

   Certainly not! She always comes up with a clever ____________ icism.

8. Jose is very competitive. He loves ____________ ition.

D. Fill in the blank with an appropriate key word.

People who are born under the sign of Gemini are usually ____________ and like change. They like excitement; they hate ____________. There is nothing ____________ about their daily life. Geminis enjoy sports because they like ____________. At parties people enjoy their company because they are ____________ and very ____________, often making clever comments. But they are very ____________. They often change partners. They are not always healthy, because they have ______________ bodies.

June 21 ↞

Cancer

↠ July 22

The symbol of Cancer is the crab. Cancerians are like the real crab in several ways. Most of them seem to have a hard shell on the outside but they are actually extremely **sensitive**. It is easy to hurt their feelings. Cancerians are **tenacious.** Like the real crab, they will not give up something that belongs to them. Their possessions are very important to them. Cancerians are not **impulsive**. They look at a situation carefully before making a decision.

Cancer's personality is, however, forever changing. They can be very **melancholy**, even very sad. At other times, they can be **humorous**. They love to laugh and tell jokes and are very optimistic, believing the future will be good. Cancer is not a **passionate** sign. They don't really love anything deeply. The only exception is their home and family. Cancerians are happiest when they are at home.

CAREER: Those born under the sign of Cancer are serious and hard-working. They excel in business and in commerce. In fact, the financial world is **fascinating** for Cancerians. Because of their great interest in possessions and money, they will rarely have money problems, as they have a special talent for making their investments grow.

LOVE: A Cancerian should avoid an Aquarian, as this sign is known to be **unfaithful**. A Cancerian would not trust them. Taureans can be quite **domestic** like Cancerians. They both enjoy home life. This sign would be one of the best choices for a Cancerian. A Pisces, another water sign, would also be **compatible**. They would get along well.

Famous Cancerians

Julius Caesar	Helen Keller	Tom Hanks
Nelson Mandela	Ariana Grande	Prince William

A. Match the phrase in column A with a phrase in column B.

A	B
1. A **fascinating** woman is _____	A) funny.
2. An **unfaithful** individual _____	B) emotional.
3. A **compatible** couple _____	C) have feelings that are easily hurt.
4. A **domestic** person _____	D) get along easily.
5. A **passionate** individual is _____	E) very interesting.
6. A **humorous** story is _____	F) enjoys being home.
7. A **melancholy** individual is _____	G) might have a secret lover.
8. An **impulsive** leader _____	H) will not give up easily.
9. A **tenacious** individual _____	I) can make decisions too quickly.
10. **Sensitive** people _____	J) sad, unhappy.

B. Complete the sentence with one of the words below.

melancholy	faithful	impulsiveness	fascinating
passion	tenacity	sensitivity	domesticity
humorous	compatible		

1. Everyone enjoys talking to _________________ people because they always have interesting things to discuss.
2. Gustav's _________________ has often gotten him into trouble. He really should think things out more carefully before making a decision.
3. Some people think Andre is stubborn. He sticks to what he believes in. He's well known for his _________________.
4. _________________people make others sad and depressed. They are not fun to be with.
5. Brigitte loves to clean house and cook. She is known for her _________________.
6. Leyla and Kamran have a perfect marriage. They are very _________________.
7. Penelope was a _______________ wife. She waited a long time for Ulysses to return.
8. Juan has a _________________for gourmet food and fine wine.
9. Harlan is so funny! His _________________ stories always make us laugh.
10. Oscar feels so sorry for all the poor, helpless people in the world. Everyone respects him for his _________________ to others.

C. Complete the sentence with the correct form of the word in bold type.

1. She liked to talk about **sensitivity**; and she herself was very ________________.
2. He had a lot of **tenacity**; he was ________________.
3. She talked a great deal about **impulsiveness**, and she was ________________herself.
4. She loved to discuss **humor**, and she was ________________herself.
5. He talked about the need for **passion**, and he was himself ________________.
6. She talked a great deal about **domesticity**, and she enjoyed being ________________.
7. His followers were very **faithful**. Not a single one was ______________.
8. The lecture was **fascinating**; the audience was ________________.

D. Fill in each blank with the correct form of the word..

1. The opposite of boring is ________________.
2. A person who will not support a friend in difficulty is ________________.
3. Hans and Ursula get along well together. They are________________.
4. A person who feels sad and depressed suffers from ________________.
5. Clowns and comedians have a good sense of ________________.
6. The opposite of slow or deliberate is ________________.
7. A person who loves or hates with deep feeling is________________.

July 23

Leo

August 22

The symbol for Leo is the lion, the king of the jungle. Like all rulers, Leos are very **dignified**. They do not do silly or cheap things. They always look very important. They are also very **proud** of themselves; they believe very strongly in their own ability and in everything they do. Some people would say they are **vain**—too proud. They are well aware of their personal worth and have a great deal of respect for themselves. Because of this, other people often think they are **egotistical**, thinking only of themselves. The fact is, Leos do care about people. Sometimes they think this gives them the right to be **domineering** – telling other people what to do, dominating them – and Leos find it difficult to take orders from others. They may hurt people's feelings because they are **honest**, and tell people the truth even if it hurts.

Leos are **materialistic** people, loving beautiful clothes, jewelry, cars, and houses. They are willing to work hard to acquire these things. but they are not **cautious** with money. They often spend more than they should. Fortunately, they are always able to find ways of paying for the things they want.

CAREER: The leadership abilities of Leos may take them into fields such as law, politics, business, and the military services.

LOVE: Leos are loyal and loving even though they tend to be **bossy**, insisting on making most of the decisions. They should avoid Arians, who may be **overpowering** and dominate them. A good partner would be a Virgo, who admires strength in others.

Famous Leos

Napoleon Bonaparte
Barack Obama
Fidel Castro
Roger Federer
Jennifer Lopez
Madonna

A. Match each phrase in column A with a phrase in column B. Some may match in two places.

A	B
1. **Honest** people _____	A) like to possess expensive things.
2. **Materialistic** people _____	B) have very strong and persuasive personalities.
3. **Cautious** people _____	C) like to tell others what to do.
4. **Bossy** people _____	D) are very careful.
5. **Egotistical** people _____	E) never lie or steal.
6. **Vain** people _____	F) think only of themselves.
7. **Dignified** people _____	G) worry about how they look.
8. **Proud** people _____	H) have a lot of self-respect.
9. **Domineering** people _____	I) think they are very important.
10. **Overpowering** people _____	J) take control of a situation.

B. Complete each sentence with one of the words below.

honesty	materialism	caution	bossy	vain
dignity	pride	dominated	overpowered	

1. Orhan takes _______________ in his skills as a chef.
2. The famous general maintained his _______________ while he was a prisoner.
3. The Manchester team _______________ its opponent.
4. A well-known saying is " _______________ is the best policy."
5. A yellow traffic light is a signal for _______________.
6. He complained that his wife was too _______________, always telling him what to do.
7. The great writer Henry Thoreau attacked _______________ – people's obsession with things.
8. The election _______________ the headlines.
9. An egotistical person is usually quite _______________.

C. Choose the correct word or expression and write it in the blank.

1. The opposite of **cautious** is ________________ (careless, careful, carefree).
2. To be **egotistical** means to be ________________ (self-centered, self-pitying, by yourself).
3. An **honest** person would never ________________ (tell a joke, tell a lie, tell the truth).
4. To **dominate** someone is to ________________ (rule them, punish them, admire them).
5. **Bossy** also means ________________ (docile, domineering, domain).
6. **Materialism** involves ________________ (places, possessions, strange things).
7. The adjective form of the noun **pride** is ________________ (proudly, proud, proudness).
8. A person who has **dignity** has ________________ (a lot of feeling, self-respect, responsibility).

D. Fill in each blank with the correct form of the word.

1. Juanita is extremely careful when she drives. She is a ________________ driver.
2. Pablo worked at two jobs in order to pay his wife's hospital bill. He was too ________________ to ask his family for help.
3. I don't like Hanna. All she cares about is herself. She is so ________________.
4. Working with Greta is very difficult. She is so ________________, always telling me what to do.
5. The poor old man was attacked and robbed of all his money; he was ________________ed by the criminals.
6. I wish you would stop looking at yourself in every mirror we pass! You are so ________________.
7. "Let's be ________________, we can't win this game."

⇠ Virgo ⇢

August 23 — September 22

The symbol for Virgo is a virgin, a woman who has not made physical love with a man. People born under the sign of Virgo want to be **perfect**. They hate mistakes so they do their work carefully and in an exact manner. It must be perfect. Because perfection is so important, sometimes they become very **anxious** – uncomfortable, worrying about the results of their work. They are very **efficient**; they do not waste time. They are also very **thrifty**; they do not like to waste money. For this reason, they are excellent employees. They are **meticulous** about their person and home; everything must be clean and neat. Virgos can forgive weakness in everyone except themselves.

Although Virgos appear to be cool and calm, they are often **nervous**. In fact, they worry a lot. However, their friends know they can rely on them for help or advice; they are **dependable**. Virgos are also known for being **gentle**. They do not want to be hurtful, and they are **compassionate**, feeling deeply for others.

CAREER: Virgos will be successful in fields that demand intelligence and efficiency. They make excellent executives or bankers.

LOVE: Taureans are relaxed people, a good choice for nervous Virgos. With Cancerians, Virgos can share love, home, family, and friends. Geminis and Aquarians are too restless for Virgos. They like change, but Virgos do not.

Famous Virgos

Queen Elizabeth I, Salma Hayek, Michael Jackson, Bill Murray, Beyonce, Prince Harry

A. Match the word or phrase in column A with a phrase in column B.

A	B
1. A **meticulous** person _____	A) is good with money.
2. A **thrifty** person _____	B) is very sympathetic.
3. A **nervous** person _____	C) is kind and not aggressive.
4. A **compassionate** person _____	D) hates mistakes.
5. A **gentle** person _____	E) can be relied on.
6. A **dependable** person _____	F) wastes time and energy.
7. An **anxious** person _____	G) is very neat.
8. An **inefficient** person _____	H) is not relaxed and calm.
9. A **perfectionist** _____	I) worries a lot.

B. Fill in each blank with the correct word.

perfectionist	meticulous	gentle	compassionate	
anxious	dependable	nervous	thrifty	efficient

1.Serap always feels sorry for people when they have problems. What a __________ person!

2. You are worrying too much about the examination. Don't be so ____________ about it.

3. My mother is a ____________housekeper. She keeps our house spotless.

4. Henri doesn't know how to organize his life. He needs to be more ____________ .

5. Juliette is in charge of the party. Everything will be ready in time. She is so ____________

6. Lee lives so well on such a small salary. What a ____________ person!

7. Alex is a ____________. He hardly ever makes mistakes.

8. Miko never loses her temper. She is so kind and sweet. She is truly a ____________ person.

9. Marta worries about everything. She is such an ______________ person.

C. Write the correct form of the word in bold type.

1. **Efficient** people are known for their _______________ cy.
2. **Anxious** people have a problem with _______________ ty.
3. **Dependable** people are known for their _______________ ity.
4. **Gentle** people are admired for their _____________ ness.
5. **Compassionate** people are known for their _______________.
6. **Nervous** people are known for their _______________ ness.
7. **Thrifty** people practice _______________ iness.
8. A **perfectionist** wants everything to be _______________.

D. Fill in the blank with the correct form of the word.

1. The opposite of calm or relaxed is _______________.
2. A person who spends money foolishly is not _______________.
3. An unfeeling individual lacks _______________ for others.
4. An _______________ expert knows a lot about how to use time wisely.
5. A person who always worries suffers from _______________ .
6. Maria believes in order and excellence. She is probably a ________________.
7. Everything must be in the right place; my mother is _______________.
8. A lamb is known for its _______________.
9. _______________ people will never let you down.

September 23 ↞

Libra

↠ October 22

The symbol for Libra is the golden scale of justice. As the purpose of scales is to balance, the personality of a Libra is well-balanced and **calm**. Libras are quiet, **gracious** people who are kind and charming. When others are fighting, Libras will play the role of peacemaker. Libras seek a **harmonious** life. They do not like arguments. They feel life is too short for people to waste their time being **nasty**—very unkind to each other. Libras will always try to be **fair**. They do not take sides in arguments; they do not favor one person more than another.

Typical Libras are sometimes accused of being **indecisive** because they take a long time to make up their minds about certain things. However, they are **logical** thinkers. They solve problems by looking at the facts. Libras are known for their clear thinking. Libras rarely suffer from serious illness. They will enjoy good health as long as they make sure to get plenty of rest. If they do not, they can be **cranky**. They will not be pleasant.

CAREER: Libras are **sensible** people. They have a lot of common sense and are capable of making **intelligent** decisions that make good sense. A Libra would make an excellent executive, but would also excel as a lawyer, a judge, or a military officer.

LOVE: Another Libra would be a good choice, because harmony and beauty are so important to them. Because beauty is so important, Libras are sometimes **extravagant.** They believe in spending money on expensive, beautiful things; but they are careful with their finances, so they can usually afford these luxuries. The worst possible choice would be Virgo. Libras dislike people who are nervous and worry too much.

Famous Libras

Mahatma Gandhi	Oscar Wilde	John Lennon
Vladimir Putin	Serena Williams	Vera Wang

A. Match the phrase in column A with a phrase in Column B.

A	B
1. People who are extravagant _____	A) thinks things out carefully.
2. A person who is cranky _____	B) can't make up their minds.
3. People who are fair _____	C) is charming and kind.
4. A sensible person _____	D) spend a lot of money.
5. A person who is logical _____	E) never gets overexcited.
6. People who are nasty _____	F) believe in justice.
7. An intelligent person _____	G) has good common sense.
8. Indecisive people _____	H) is unpleasant.
9. A person who is gracious_____	I) is very smart.
10. A person who is calm _____	J) are very disagreeable.

B. Complete each sentence with one of the words below.

extravagance	logical	sense	nastiness
fairness	indecisive	calmness	crankiness
graciousness	intelligent		

1. The judge is known for his honesty and ______________. He never takes sides.
2. Marta is such a charming hostess. We always enjoy her parties. She's famous for her ______________.
3. An ______________ decision usually results in success.
4. Marco said some terrible things about me last night. His ______________ really hurt me.
5. Buying a sports car is a true ______________ . They are so expensive!
6. Kaori never gets upset when there is a crisis. She is well known for her ______________.
7. Liam's reasoning didn't make any sense. He wasn't ______________!
8. I avoid my roommate in the morning – he is so unpleasant.

   His ______________ gets on my nerves!
9. Every time I speak to Manuel he has changed his plans. What an ______________ person!
10. I'm glad I have a friend like Serap. I come up with some crazy ideas, but her good ______________ always helps me make the right decision.

C. Fill in the blank with the correct form of the word in bold type.

1. **Calm** people are known for their ____________ .
2. **Gracious** people are known for their ____________ .
3. **Intelligent** people are known for their ____________ .
4. **Nasty** people are known for their ____________ .
5. **Logical** people think ____________ .
6. A **fair** person is known for their _____________ .
7. **Sensible** people are known for their common ____________ .
8. **Cranky** people are known for their ____________ .
9. **Extravagant** people are known for their ____________ .
10. **Indecisive** people are known for their ____________ .

D. In the blanks, write the opposites of the words in bold type.

1. Anita was **upset**. _____________
2. Pierre is so **thrifty**. _____________
3. The officer was very **decisive**. _____________
4. Arturo is a **happy, pleasant** person. _____________
5. His thinking was **illogical**. _____________
6. That was a really **stupid** thing to do. _____________
7. His words were **kind**. _____________
8. He is **not charming**. _____________
9. She is often **sweet and pleasant**. _____________

October 23 ⇠

Scorpio

⇢ November 21

The symbol of Scorpio is the scorpion. The scorpion has a poisonous sting that can sometimes kill the victim. Like the scorpion, Scorpios can be **brutal** to their enemies. They can cause serious injury. However, they react this way only when attacked or hurt. Like Arians, they are not aggressive, but they are **courageous**. They are not afraid of anything, because they are **confident** people. They believe they are capable of accomplishing whatever they set out to do.

Scorpios are passionate people with **intense be**liefs. They can be very **emotional**. However, they will work hard to not show their feelings. Therefore, few people ever know them well, because they are so **secretive.** Scorpios know how to control themselves, and they will never tell a lot about themselves.

CAREER: They are very **smart**, and also very **talented**. They can excel in a variety of fields such as politics, entertainment, and religion.

LOVE: Scorpios should avoid Leos, who will try to dominate them. Another Scorpio will make them **jealous**; they may think the other person will cheat on them with another lover. People born under the calmer signs such as Libra or Taurus would be better for Scorpios.

Famous Scorpios

Prince Charles	Whoopi Goldberg	Pablo Picasso
Marie Curie	Hillary Rodham Clinton	Bill Gates

A. Match the key word in column A with a phrase in column B.

A	B
1. **Brutal** people_____	A) are strong and brave.
2. **Courageous** people _____	B) have many skills.
3. **Confident** people _____	C) don't trust their partners.
4. **Intense** people _____	D) are very intelligent.
5. **Secretive** people _____	E) are not calm and relaxed.
6. **Emotional** people _____	F) believe in themselves.
7. **Smart** people _____	G) rarely talk about themselves.
8. **Jealous** people _____	H) have very strong feelings.
9. **Talented** people _____	I) may hurt others very badly.

B. Complete each sentence with one of the words below.

emotionally	secretly	confident
brutally	courageously	intense
jealousy	smart	talented

1. Her boyfriend's_______________ caused her to leave him.
2. His _______________ need was to be a millionaire.
3. The prison guard _______________ punished the prisoner.
4. He was _______________ that he would get the job.
5. I didn't trust him, because he _______________ kept the truth to himself.
6. He was in pain, but he _______________ kept trying to win.
7. That little boy is very _______________. He reads everything.
8. She is a very _______________ violinist.
9. The teacher reacted very _______________. She started to cry.

C. Fill in the blank with the correct form of the key word.

1. Her husband was very **jealous**. His _______________ angered her.
2. Our enemies are very **brutal**. Their _______________ was awful.
3. Our children are very **confident**. Their _______________ is impressive.
4. They have too many **secrets**. Our friends are very _______________.
5. Our teachers are very **intense**. They teach with amazing _______________.
6. He did not like to show **emotion**, but he got very _______________ over the death of his dog.
7. She had many **talents**. She was very _______________.
8. Our soldiers are very **courageous**. Their _______________ saved us.

D. Fill in the blank with the correct form of a key word.

1. The president is too _______________; he should be calmer.
2. That was a bad decision; I don't think she's very _______________.
3. He loves to sing, but really he is not very _______________.
4. Someone who is fearful is not _______________.
5. A spy or a detective is usually a _______________ person.
6. Murderers can be very _______________.
7. Someone who is afraid of losing a friend is a _______________ person.
8. A person who has passionate beliefs is _______________ .
9. People who don't feel they can do well at anything aren't _______________.

Sagittarius

November 22 – December 21

The symbol for Sagittarius is the Archer. Sagittarius is the most honest and truthful sign of the zodiac. Some people may even consider Sagittarians **blunt** because they always tell the truth even if it hurts. They have lots of loyal friends because they are almost always **cheerful** and **friendly**. They are rarely unhappy and love to talk to everyone. Sagittarians find it difficult to take life too seriously.They are never **pessimistic** about life. Sagittarians believe that tomorrow will be even better than today.

Sagittarians love **exciting** activities. They love to drive fast cars or to climb mountains. **Boring** activities are not for them. Their lives are always interesting. Sagittarians are **fearless**. There is nothing that they are afraid to do. They have **imaginative**, very creative minds, full of thoughts and ideas. They are very **clever** and often come up with new ideas. They avoid being responsible for something, such as being in charge of organizations and other people.

CAREER: Those born under the sign of Sagittarius love to be surrounded by people and excitement. They are often found in fields such as show business, teaching, aviation, and politics.

LOVE: Sagittarians love to travel; so a fellow Sagittarian would be perfect. A loving and intelligent Libra would also be a good partner. Sagittarians should forget Scorpios, however, because Scorpios are too jealous and would try to control them.

Famous Sagittarians

Ludwig van Beethoven
Winston Churchill
Emmanuel Macron
Brad Pitt
Miley Cyrus
Caroline Kennedy

A. Match the phrase in column A with the best phrase in column B.

A	B
1. **Responsible** people ______	A) attracts attention.
2. An **imaginative** person ______	B) is quite intelligent.
3. A **clever** individual ______	C) enjoy meeting new people.
4. **Fearless** people ______	D) feel the future will be bad.
5. A **boring** person ______	E) is sometimes too honest.
6. An **exciting** personality ______	F) smiles and laughs a lot.
7. **Pessimistic** people ______	G) are not afraid of anything.
8. **Friendly** people ______	H) take good care of their family.
9. A **cheerful** person ______	I) thinks of new ways to do things.
10. A **blunt** person ______	J) is not very interesting.

B. Complete each of the sentences with one of the words below.

excitement	friendliness	responsibility	imagination	fearlessness
boredom	pessimism	cheerfulness	blunt	clever

1. It is good to tell the truth, but being _____________ can hurt people's feelings.
2. Parents have the _____________ of raising their children.
3. Her _____________ makes us feel better even when times are bad.
4. The _____________ of our neighbors made us happy to be a part of the community.
5. His _____________ makes everyone feel sad and depressed.
6. We enjoyed the _____________ of the circus.
7. The _____________ of doing exactly the same thing every day drove us crazy.
8. The soldier was given a special award for his _____________ in battle.
9. Being _____________ at business made him a millionaire.
10. Walt Disney used great _____________ to design Disneyland.

C. Write the correct form of the word in bold type.

1. **Blunt** people often speak too _____________.
2. **Cheerful** people are known for their _____________.
3. **Friendly** animals are loved for their _____________.
4. **Pessimistic** people seem to enjoy their _____________.
5. **Exciting** events create _____________.
6. **Clever** people are known for their _____________.
7. **Fearless** people are admired for their _____________.
8. **Imaginative** artists are known for their wonderful _____________.
9. **Boring** jobs cause _____________ .
10. **Responsible** people always accept _____________ .

D. Fill in the blanks with the correct form of the key words.

1. A person who is always happy is _____________.
2. The opposite of optimistic is _____________.
3. Someone who is too shy to start a conversation is usually not _____________.
4. The opposite of interesting is _____________.
5. A person who is creative is _____________.
6. Someone who is never afraid is _____________.
7. The opposite of stupid is _____________.
8. A person who never gets to work on time is not _____________.
9. Someone who tells the absolute truth at all times is _____________.
10. A football game can be very _____________.

December 22

Capricorn

January 19

The symbol for Capricorn is the determined goat, who is constantly climbing upward. Capricorns are very **serious** about life. They think and plan for the future carefully. They are very ambitious and **diligent**, working long, hard hours and rarely making mistakes. Capricorns may seem **tough**, strong and not easily hurt, but they really have kind hearts. Some people may consider them **snobbish** because they admire successful people and like to associate with them.

Capricorns are **conservative** about the way they dress. They will not wear bright colors or anything unusual. At times they may appear to be **shy** because they are quiet people. They are not unfriendly; they prefer to listen. Capricorns know they can learn a lot from other people. They are **disciplined** people who have great self-control and accomplish what they set out to do.

CAREER: Capricorns are **practical** people. Their ideas make sense and are useful. For this reason they are successful in most fields. They are found most often in the business world.

LOVE: A Taurean would make a good mate. Those born under the sign of Taurus are determined and home-loving. A Leo and a Capricorn would get along well because of their mutual love of success and money. Those born under the signs of Aries and Sagittarius are not **stable** enough. They tend to be restless and changeable.

Famous Capricorns

Joan of Arc　Mao Tse-tung　Denzel Washington　Michelle Obama
Martin Luther King, Jr.　Kate Middleton (Duchess of Cambridge)

A. Match each phrase in column A with the best phrase in column B.

A	B
1. **Practical** people______	A) are timid and quiet.
2. **Stable** people ______	B) think they are better than other people.
3. **Disciplined** people______	C) worry about new ideas and change.
4. **Shy** people ______	D) are hard-working.
5. **Conservative** people______	E) are not easily upset.
6. **Snobbish** people ______	F) are strong and and not easily hurt.
7. **Tough** people______	G) don't do silly things.
8. **Diligent** people ______	H) think and plan carefully.
9. **Serious** people ______	I) have control over their own lives.

B. Complete each of the following sentences with a form of one of the key words below.

practicality	shy	toughness
stability	conservatism	diligence
discipline	snobbishness	serious

1. Christine is often restless. Her brother is the opposite. He's known for his _______________.
2. Mustafa is an excellent employee. His work is always finished ahead of time. He's known for his _______________.
3. Alvino has always spent most of his time studying and planning for the future. He's known for being _______________ .
4. Astrid has a difficult time making friends. She's known for being _______________.
5. Mariko never wastes money or food. She's known for her _______________.
6. Hugo will only become friends with people who are rich and powerful. He's known for his _______________.
7. Max is the opposite of liberal. He's known for his _______________ .
8. Giles never forgets to do his homework or clean his room. He jogs three miles a day and has a part-time job. He's known for his self- _______________ .
9. In the old West, people had to be strong. Those people were known for their _______________.

C. Fill in each blank with the correct form of the word in bold type.

1. Although he was a **serious** person, he didn't always show his _______________ .
2. Although he was a **diligent** person, he didn't always show his _______________ .
3. Although he was a **tough** person, he didn't always show his _______________ .
4. Although he was a **snobbish** person, he didn't always show his _______________ .
5. Although he was a **conservative** person, he didn't always show his _______________ .
6. Although he was a **shy** person, he didn't always show his _______________ .
7. Although he was a **disciplined** person, he didn't always show his _______________ .
8. Although he was an **unstable** person, he didn't always show his _______________ .

D. Fill in the blanks with the correct form of the key words.

1. He's always telling jokes and laughing. He's certainly not _______________ .
2. Someone who has common sense is usually quite _______________ .
3. She was put into a mental institution because she was very _______________ .
4. A person who never gets anything done on time may lack _______________ .
5. The opposite of being silly is being _______________ .
6. The opposite of liberal is _______________.
7. People who think they are superior are _______________ ,
8. The opposite of weak is _______________ .
9. A lazy person is not _______________ .

January 20

Aquarius

February 18

The symbol for Aquarius is the water carrier. Aquarians are kind and likeable, but sometimes they appear to be **aloof**. They may seem distant and disinterested in the people around them. They do not have many close friends. However, once they develop a friendship, they will always be **loyal**. Aquarians will always help a friend in trouble or in need. They are extremely **curious** about their friends, insisting on knowing everything about them.

Typical Aquarians are **unconventional**, different from everyone else. They will often refuse to do what society expects them to do. At times, they are even **eccentric**, doing very unusual things. They may wear jeans to a formal dinner and keep an alligator as a pet. Because of this behavior, they are known to be **unpredictable**. No one knows what they will do next. Aquarians like being **independent**. If someone tries to stop them from doing what they enjoy, they become unhappy or even angry. Aquarius is the sign of genius. They are **creative**, capable of producing new ideas and inventing unusual things. They possess the most outstanding intellect of all the signs of the zodiac. They are known for being **wise**.

***CAREER**:* Aquarians' intellect and creative talents will probably lead them into fields such as writing, science, acting, or even astrology.

***LOVE**:* Excellent partners are Capricorns, who will not try to possess Aquarians, allowing them the freedom they need. Leos, another choice, like people who are **creative** and intelligent, like Aquarians. They should avoid Scorpios, whose **critical** comments will hurt them. Aquarians do not like to be told constantly that what they are doing is wrong.

Famous Aquarians

Abraham Lincoln, Charles Darwin, Alice Walker
Oprah Winfrey, Wolfgang A. Mozart, Babe Ruth, Justin Timberlake

A. Match each phrase in column A with a phrase in column B.

A	B
1. A **curious** person ______	A) likes to be free.
2. An **unconventional** person is______	B) very intelligent.
3. An **eccentric** person ______	C) unfriendly.
4. A **loyal** friend is ______	D) likes to learn new things.
5. A **critical** person is someone who ______	E) finds new ways to do things.
6. A **creative** person ______	F) different from most people.
7. A **wise** person is______	G) a faithful friend.
8. An **aloof** person is ______	H) often does unexpected things.
9. An **unpredictable** person ______	I) often says negative things.
10. An **independent** person ______	J) does strange or unusual things.

B. Fill in the blanks.

curiosity	loyalty	wisdom	unconventional
criticism	aloofness	eccentric	creativity
unpredictable	independence		

1. Therese will always be my best friend. When I was very sick, she came to the hospital every day.Therese is known for her _______________.
2. Marko can sometimes be very difficult. Yesterday he laughed and told jokes all day. Today he seems sad and depressed. What is wrong with him? Marko is extremely _______________.
3. Katarina refuses to accept help from anyone. She prefers to do things her way and to do them when she feels like it. She is known for her _______________.
4. Ivan is usually a nice person but sometimes his mind seems so far away. At times, he doesn't even speak when we meet. Ivan is known for his _______________.
5. Anastasia is interested in everything. She always asks questions about things. Anastasia has a lot of _______________.
6. Sometimes Carlos really hurts me. He constantly tells me that I'm wrong or that he doesn't like my clothes. I don't like harsh _______________.
7. The pictures you draw are so original. You are so imaginative. I'm so impressed with your _______________!
8. We should listen to old people who have lived a long time and had a lot of experience. They often have a lot more _______________ than we do.
9. Boris is very _______________. He always does things in a different way.
10. _______________ people are so different, other people may think they are crazy.

C. Write the correct form of the word in bold type.

1. **Curious** people are known for their _______________.
2. **Loyal** people are known for their _______________.
3. **Critical** people are known for their _______________.
4. **Independent** people are known for their _______________.
5. **Creative** people are known for their _______________.
6. **Wise** people are known for their ______________.
7. **Eccentric** people are known for their ________________.

D. Fill in each blank with the correct form of the word.

Aquarians are sometimes disliked for their _______________, because they aren't always friendly. Actually, they are quite _______________ about their friends and the world around them. Aquarians are occasionally ____________, doing things that are unexpected. They are very intelligent, but unconventional and _______________, sometimes a little strange. People born under the sign of Aquarius love their freedom and _______________. One thing Aquarians don't like is _______________; it hurts them very much. Above all, they are respected for their intellect and _______________.

February 19

Pisces

March 20

The symbol for gentle Pisces is the fish. Pisceans have **tender** hearts. They are kind and understanding to anyone with problems. Pisces is the most **altruistic** sign of the zodiac. They help others and expect nothing in return. Pisceans are not **selfish**. Pisceans have little interest in money. They spend their money as fast as they make it. Pisceans do not want what other people have. They aren't **envious**. They will share whatever they have. Pisceans may seem **timid**, because they are quiet people. In reality, they enjoy being with people very much.

Pisceans aren't at all **greedy**. Material possessions mean little to them; they will give their things away to others. Pisceans find their greatest pleasure in the beauty of nature and friendship. People are attracted to them because of their **tranquil** ways. It is almost impossible to make them angry or upset. They are **indifferent** to opinions that they do not agree with. Pisceans pay no attention to insults, although they can be hurt by unkind remarks if they are true. They prefer to live in the dream-like undersea world.

CAREER: Pisceans love art and music. Many actors, musicians, and artists are born under this sign.

LOVE: Taureans are a good choice for Pisceans. Pisceans can be lazy. They do not like to work. Taureans are hard workers and good at saving money. They will also share a love of beauty and nature. Sagittarians should be avoided. This sign can be very **frank**. Pisceans' feelings can be hurt by criticism if it is true.

Famous Pisceans

George Washington
Michelangelo
Auguste Renoir
Javier Bardem
Amy Tan
Gabriel García Márquez

A. Match the phrase in column A with a phrase in column B.

A	B
1. A greedy person ______	A) speaks openly and honestly.
2. A timid person is ______	B) quiet or serene.
3. A tranquil person is ______	C) kind and gentle.
4. A person with a tender heart is	D) to put others or other things above self.
5. To be altruistic is ______	E) to not show interest.
6. A selfish person ______	F) shy or unfriendly.
7. To be indifferent is ______	G) does not like to share.
8. A frank person ______	H) is to want what someone else has.
9. To be envious ______	I) wants more than they need.

B. Fill in each blank with a form of one of these words.

tenderness	indifference	tranquility
frankness	timidity	envious
selfishness	greediness	altruism

1. He eats like a pig! His _______________ really gets on my nerves.
2. I wish I had long blonde hair like Ursula. I'm really _______________ of her.
3. Yesterday Heinrich told me that my dress was ugly. His _______________ hurt me.
4. Marta is so quiet around people. Her _______________ prevents her from making friends.
5. Jaime told me that it didn't make any difference to him what we plan for the weekend. His _______________ makes me feel that he doesn't want to be with us.
6. I love the city but sometimes it's so noisy! The _______________ and beauty of the country is so restful.
7. He has so few friends because all he cares about is himself. His _______________ is the worst thing about him.
8. She's such a kind and gentle nurse. Her patients love her for her _______________.
9. Although he is a millionaire he gives a lot of his money to help the poor. He is famous for his _______________.

C. Write the adverb (-ly) form of the word in bold type.

1. **Greedy** people will take what they can ____________ily.
2. **Timid** people sometimes behave ____________ with strong people.
3. **Tranquil** people often react to problems ____________.
4. **Tender** people are known to treat those in pain ____________.
5. **Selfish** people often act ____________.
6. **Indifferent** people often react ____________.
7. **Frank** people often speak ____________.

D. Fill in the blanks with the correct form of the words.

1. A person who does not like to share with others is ____________.
2. It is good to be honest but some people are too ____________.
3. A person who doesn't have much interest or desire to learn about a particular subject is ____________ to it.
4. The opposite of generosity or giving is ____________.
5. People who give up a comfortable life to help others are ____________ individuals.
6. Treating people roughly is the opposite of treating them ____________.
7. After a bad storm the sea is calm and ____________.
8. Shy is similar in meaning to ____________.
9. People who take more food than they need are ____________.

Answers

Aries, p. 2
A
1 – B
2 – I
3 – H
4 – A
5 – C
6 – K
7 – G
8 – F
9 -- J
10 – D
11 – E

B
1.decisive
2. energetic
3. ambitious
4. sympathetic
5. impatient
6. optimistic
7. combative
8. aggressive
9. brash
10. enthusiastic

C
1. energy
2. sympathy
3. aggressiveness
4. combat
5. optimism
6. impatience
7. brashness
8. enthusiasm
9.ambition
10. decisiveness

D
1. I
2. H
3. E
4. K
5. G
6. J
7. B
8. C
9. F
10. D
11. A

Taurus, p. 6
A
1. D
2. G
3. E
4. A
5. H
6. B
7. I
8. C
9. F

B
1. stubbornness
2. determined
3. generosity
4. obese
5. stingy
6. serenity
7. strength
8. deliberate
9. healthy

C
1. stinginess
2. obesity
3. deliberation
4. serenity
5. generosity
6. stubbornness
7. determination
8. strength
9. health

D
1. G
2. E
3. F
4. C
5. A
6. B
7. D

Gemini, p. 10
A
1. D
2. E
3. A
4. C
5. I
6. G
7. B
8. F
9.H

B
1. fickle
2. witty
3. malicious
4. monotonous
5. restless
6. delicate
7. mundane
8. charming
9. competitive

C
1. fickleness
2. monotonous
3. restlessness
4. maliciouness
5. charming
6. delicateness
7. witticism
8. competition.

D
restless
monotony
mundane
competition
charming
witty
fickle
delicate

Cancer, p. 14
A
1. E
2. G
3. D
4. F
5. B
6. A
7. J
8. I
9. H
10. C

B
1. fascinating
2. impulsiveness
3. tenacity
4. melancholy
5. domesticity
6. compatible
7. faithful
8. passion
9. humorous
10. sensitivity

C
1. sensitive
2. tenacious
3. impulsive
4. humorous
5. passionate
6. domestic
7. unfaithful
8. fascinated

D
1. fascinating
2. unfaithful
3. compatible
4. melancholy
5. humor
6. impulsive
7. passionate

Leo, p. 18

A
1. E
2. A
3. D
4. C, J
5. F
6. G
7. H, I
8. I, H
9. J, C
10. B

B
1. pride
2. dignity
3. overpowered, dominated
4. honesty
5. caution
6. bossy
7. materialism
8. dominated
9. vain

C
1. careless
2. self-centered
3. tell a lie
4. rule them
5. domineering
6. possessions
7. proud
8. self-respect

D
1. cautious
2. proud
3. egotistical
4. bossy, domineering
5. overpowered
6. vain
7. honest

Virgo, p. 22

A
1. G
2. A
3. H
4. B
5. C
6. E
7. I
8. F
9. D, G

B
1. sympathetic
2. nervous, anxious
3. meticulous
4. efficient
5. dependable
6. thrifty
7. perfectionist
8. gentle
9. anxious

C
1. efficiency
2. anxiety
3. dependability
4. gentleness
5. compassion
6. nervousness
7. thriftiness
8. perfect

D
1. nervous
2. thrifty
3. compassion
4. efficiency
5. anxiety
6. perfectionist
7. meticulous
8. gentleness
9. dependable

Libra. p. 26

A
1. D
2. H
3. F
4. G
5. A
6. J
7. I
8. B
9. C
10. E

B
1. fairness
2. graciousness
3. intelligent
4. nastiness
5. extravagance
6. calmness
7. logical
8. crankiness
9. indecisive
10. sense

C
1. calmness
2. graciousness
3. intelligence
4. nastiness
5. logically
6. fairness
7. sense
8. crankiness
9. extravagance
10. indecisiveness

D
1. calm
2. extravagant
3. indecisive
4. nasty, cranky
5. logical
6. intelligent
7. nasty
8. gracious
9. cranky

Scorpio, p. 30

A
1. I
2. A
3. F
4. E
5. G
6. H
7. D
8. C
9. B

B
1. jealousy
2. intense
3. brutally
4. confident
5. secretly
6. courageously
7. smart
8. talented
9. emotionally

Capricorn

C
1. jealousy
2. brutality
3. confidence
4. secretive
5. intensity
6. emotional
7. talented
8. courage

D
1. emotional
2. smart
3. talented
4. courageous
5. secretive
6. brutal
7. jealous
8. intense
9. confident

Sagittarius, p. 34

A
1. H
2. I
3. B
4. G
5. J
6. A
7. D
8. C
9. F
10. E

B
1. blunt
2. responsibility
3. cheerfulness
4. friendliness
5. pessimism
6. excitement
7. boredom
8. fearlessness
9. clever
10. imagination

C
1. bluntly
2. cheerfulness
3. friendliness
4. pessimism
5. excitement
6. cleverness
7. fearlessness
8. imagination
9. boredom
10. responsibility

D
1. cheerful
2. pessimistic
3. interesting
4. boring
5. imaginative
6. fearless
7. clever
8. responsible
9. blunt
10.exciting

Capricorn, p. 38

A
1. H
2. E
3. I
4. A
5. C
6. B
7. F
8. D
9. G

B
1. stability
2. diligence
3. serious
4. shy
5. practicality
6. snobbishness
7. conservatism
8. discipline
9. toughness

C
1. seriousness
2. diligence
3. toughness
4. snobbishness
5. conservatism
6. shyness
7. discipline
8. instability

D
1. shy
2. practical
3. unstable
4. discipline
5. serious
6. conservative
7. snobbish
8. tough
9. diligent

Aquarius, p. 42
A
1. D
2. F
3. J
4. G
5. I
6. E
7. B
8. C
9. H
10. A

B
1. loyalty
2. unpredictable
3. independence
4. aloofness
5. curiosity
6. criticism
7. imaginative, creativity
8. wisdom
9. unconventional
10. eccentric

C
1. curiosity
2. loyalty
3. criticism
4. independencc
5. creativity
6. wisdom
7. eccentricity

D
aloofness
curious
unpredictable
eccentric
independence
criticism
wisdom

Pisces, p. 46
A
1. I
2. F
3. B
4. C
5. D
6. G
7. E
8. A
9. H

B
1. greediness
2. envious
3. frankness
4. timidity
5. indifference
6. tranquility
7. selfishness
8. tenderness
9. altruism

C
1. greedily
2. timidly
3. tranquilly
4. tenderly
5. selfishly
6. indifferently
7. frankly

D
1. selfish
2. frank
3. indifferent
4. greed
5. altruistic
6. tenderly
7. tranquil
8. timid
9. greedy, selfish

APPENDICES

Conversation Activities

To supplement the lessons for vocabulary development, conversation activities can be carried out using the following pages.

My Classmates can be used to list and talk about who was born under which sign and how they compare to the descriptions of the sign. After the very first unit, hand out "My Classmates" and have everyone tell which sign is theirs. They write down the information. Then after each unit is completed, the students can discuss the appropriateness of the sign for the featured student.

The Horoscope for Today can be used for "fortune-telling." Horoscopes can readily be found in newspapers and on the internet. Ask each student to choose a sign and write down the brief horoscope. Then they can share their horoscope with the rest of the class.

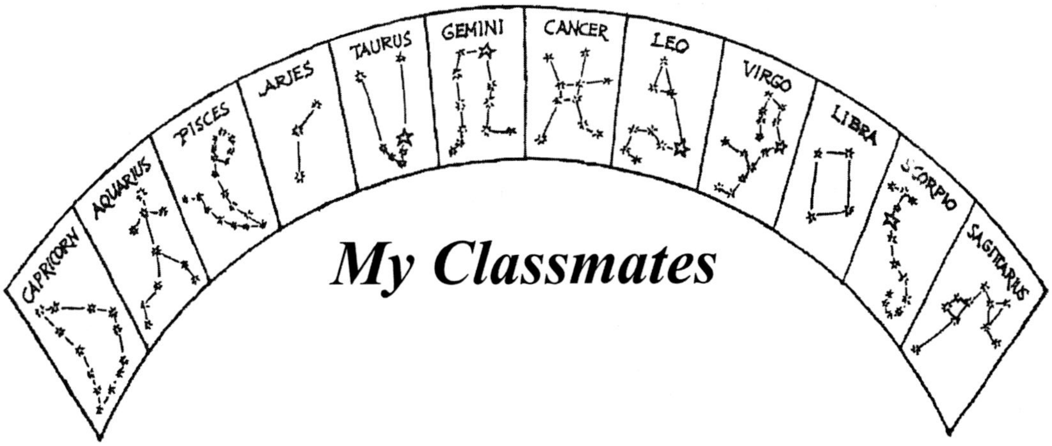

My Classmates

ARIES:

TAURUS:

GEMINI:

CANCER:

LEO:

VIRGO:

LIBRA:

SCORPIO:

SAGITTARIUS:

CAPRICORN:

AQUARIUS:

PISCES:

The Horoscope for Today:

__/__/20__

ARIES:

TAURUS:

GEMINI:

CANCER:

LEO:

VIRGO:

LIBRA:

SCORPIO:

SAGITTARIUS:

CAPRICORN:

AQUARIUS:

PISCES:

Index

The Chinese Zodiac

The Chinese Zodiac, like the one presented in this book, is related to the time of one's birth. However, unlike the Western Zodiac, which is based on the lunar month, the Chinese Zodiac is based on the year of one's birth. The Chinese Zodiac has 12 signs. Each sign (year) is linked with a personality type and named for an animal. The list of the signs below also indicates the years for that sign.

RAT	1960	1972	1984	1996	2008	2020
OX	1961	1973	1985	1997	2009	2021
TIGER	1962	1974	1986	1998	2010	2022
RABBIT	1963	1975	1987	1999	2011	2023
DRAGON	1964	1976	1988	2000	2012	2024
SNAKE	1965	1977	1989	2001	2013	2025
HORSE	1966	1978	1990	2002	2014	2026
GOAT	1967	1979	1991	2003	2015	2027
MONKEY	1968	1980	1992	2004	2016	2028
ROOSTER	1969	1981	1993	2005	2017	2029
DOG	1970	1982	1994	2006	2018	2030
PIG	1971	1983	1995	2007	2019	2031

EXAMPLE: 2020 is the year of the Rat.

If you were born in 1982, you were born in the year of the Dog.

Note that the beginning of the Chinese year is not January 1. The exact date varies from year to year according to the lunar calendar. For example. the 2018 year of the DOG begins on February 16 and ends on February 4, 2019.

To find the exact year of your birth, go to one of several websites that will calculate that for you.

A good source is: www.travelchinaguide.com/intro/social_customs/zodiac/

Note: Comparing and contrasting the ancient Western (Babylonian/Hellenistic) Zodiac with the Chinese (called Junishi in Japan) and their significance in modern Euro/North American culture and in other cultures around the world is an interesting and revealing subject for research, writing, and discussion. And there are other "zodiacs" to research. Among them are the Meso-American/Mayan/Aztec Zodiac, the African Zodiacs, Jyotisha (Hindu/Nepalese astrology), and Native American Astrology with its animal spirits and totems. Indigenous peoples throughout Eurasia, Africa, and the Americas, north and south, have similar astrological systems. Why? How old are they?

OTHER VOCABULARY DEVELOPMENT BOOKS

American Holidays.* 20 units/holidays. 195 words exploring traditions, customs, and backgrounds of the holidays. Audio CD available.

Potluck. Exploring North American Meals, Culinary Practices, and Places. 24 Units. 288 key words. 2 audio CDs available.

Wheels and Wings.143 key words associated with the world of transportation and travel.

Money. The Vocabulary of the Financial World

Shopping (under development)

OTHER BOOKS ON VOCABULARY

Lexicarry.* Pictures for Learning Languages. Over 4500 everyday words and expressions. Word lists is twelve languages correlated with the drawings.

Getting a Fix on Vocabulary: A student text that focuses on affixation. Includes all the common prefixes and suffixes and the most common bases. Text also includes "radio news" on audio CD.

The Learner's Lexicon. A word frequency list of 2400 words, divided into 300-, 600-, 1200-, and 2400-word lists.

Got It! Vocabulary games where teams compete to come up with words that are associated with lexical sets – work, food, body, weather, etc.

Go Fish. Seven beginning-level card games that focus on the basic vocabulary of the home (86 words).

Coloring in English. Beginning-level vocabulary-building coloring book for kids and adults. 40 pictures; 400 words.

A-Z Picture Activities.* Phonics and Vocabulary for Emerging Readers. One unit for each letter of the alphabet. Dozens of pictures. Audio CD available.

The Idiom Book.* 1001 Idioms in Two-Page Lessons. Based on everyday events. 2 audio CDs available.

A Phrasal Verb Affair.* 250 phrasal verbs from "add up to" to "zero in on" in a soap opera of 15 episodes. Audio CD available.

*Available as eBook/digital editions